Get It Done Now!

Binding a Quilt by Machine
2nd Edition

Ebony Love

Table of Contents

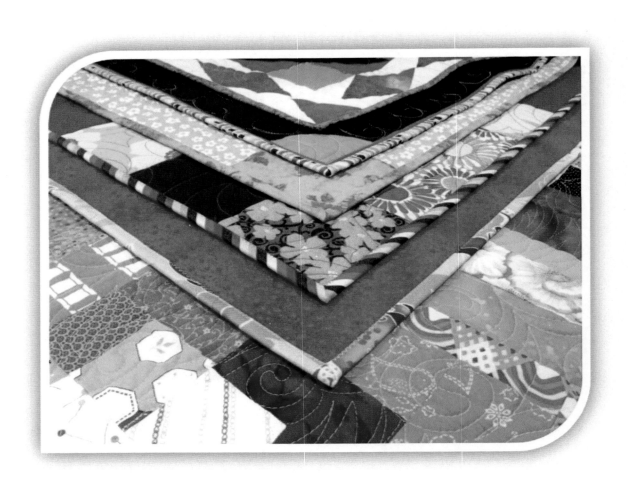

Introduction

I have so many ideas for quilts I want to make, and so little time in which to make them, that sitting down with the quilt puddled in my lap to bind by hand is a luxury I can no longer afford.

There's no denying that binding finished by hand has an irresistible appeal, but not everyone has the time or patience to finish every quilt that way. To be honest, not every quilt needs it either! Developing this binding technique was essential for me to make more quilts, meet deadlines, and still have a beautiful, professional finish.

I have a funny story from early in my teaching career. Holice Turnbow, who is an accomplished quilter and certified judge, audited one of my binding classes. As my class samples were being passed around, I told the room that this technique was great for fast finishes, but if they planned to enter shows, they should stick to hand-finished bindings.

Holice spoke up and said, "You know Ebony, I've been looking at your quilts, and I don't see any problem with using this binding in a judged show." What high praise coming from such a distinguished personage! That proud feeling quickly turned to dismay when he quipped, "Your piecing, on the other hand, would **not** win any prizes."

Since then, I've managed to improve both my piecing and binding, and I'm so thrilled to share with you the 2nd Edition of one of my most popular techniques. You'll learn to prepare your binding, attach it correctly, and finish it in a fraction of the time it usually takes— all stitched from the front of your project.

Part 1: Binding Supplies

There are so many tools on the market for binding, and no doubt you'll find your favorites as you experiment with different ways to finish your quilts. There are a few tools that I use almost all the time, and they are useful to have when using this binding technique. Check the Resources section for where to purchase.

Pins, Needles, and Thread

The quality of what holds your quilts together, both temporarily and permanently, is so important to getting a neat finish for your binding.

Clover 1½" Patchwork Glasshead Pins

These extra-fine pins pass through fabric cleanly and don't cause additional bulk.

Because the pins are so thin, you can stitch over them more safely than a bulkier pin. If you do hit one while stitching, you're more likely to bend or break the pin than the needle. You may want a spare pack of these!

One tool you won't see here are binding clips. There's nothing wrong with them in general, but many of the ones on the market are too thick to pass under the presser foot. This means you have to remove them before your project is secured by the foot and the feed dogs, and that will likely cause the binding to shift. I love binding clips for other things; just not this technique!

Schmetz 75/11 or 90/14 Quilting Needles

Size 75/11 can be used to attach the binding to the quilt, but once you turn the binding to the back, the larger 90/14 needle helps penetrate the thick layers.

The special tapered shape of the needle also works to eliminate skipped stitches.

Purchase these in bulk to increase the odds of changing your needle!

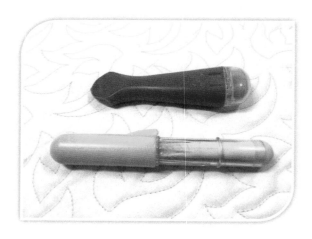

Aurifil 50wt Cotton Mako Thread

Use a neutral colored thread for basting and stitching the binding to the quilt.

To finish the binding, a matching thread is better to reduce the visibility of your stitching and blend into the binding fabric. A small 200m spool is usually sufficient to finish the binding on even a king-sized quilt.

Marking and Measuring

With the right supplies, binding your quilts becomes almost a ritual. Marking and measuring accurately during the process keeps everything square and accurate.

Clover Chaco Liner Chalk

These fine-line chalk markers work great in combination with a straight line ruler, and dispense just the right amount of chalk.

Keep a light and dark chalk on hand for visibility on a variety of fabrics.

LoveBug Studios Binding Tool

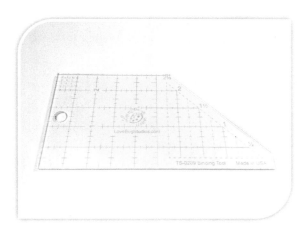

I formerly used two rulers to accomplish this technique, until necessity finally drove me to create my own binding tool.

The angled, dog-eared side helps for mitering strips and connecting the tails of the binding, while the square side aids in turning corners and measuring the overlap to finish stitching the binding to the quilt.

If you do not have this tool, you can substitute a 4½" Easy Angle Ruler and a 2½" Square Ruler.

There are many binding tools on the market, but most are focused on cutting the strips and mitering the seams. The tool I developed can be used throughout the process. It's small enough to keep at your machine, and the ⅛" markings along the ruler make it a versatile tool for marking and measuring. It can also be used as a braid template or to cut small half-square triangles from 2½" or smaller strips.

Sewing Machine

You don't need a top-of-the-line $10,000 sewing machine to get great results using this technique. There are some features that will be helpful for you to have, and this will vary by the type of machine you are using.

Vintage or Industrial Machine

Many vintage and industrial machines are uniquely different from other domestic machines in that they are only capable of doing a single type of stitch: straight!

These machines will typically only have the ability to stitch forward and reverse, with an adjustable stitch length. However, you won't be able to change the needle position, or automatically stop with the needle in a specific position.

Can you still use the techniques here with one of these machines? Yes, but you will need to make accommodations for that equipment. Instead of being able to position the needle, you will have to mark guides on your throat plate. You'll need to follow instructions for setting up your binding for straight stitching as well. Specialty feet may not be available, and you'd have to make accommodations for that too.

Personally, I think you'll have an easier time learning this technique using a more modern, domestic sewing machine.

Modern or Domestic Sewing Machine

Modern (domestic) machines are capable of performing both straight stitches and at least a zigzag stitch. You'll be able to stitch forward and backward, and the needle will also be able to move side to side. Because of this feature, your machine may also have the ability to change the position of the needle over the throat plate. At a minimum, these two features will help you the most.

If your machine has any or all of these additional features, you will have an easier time learning this technique as detailed in this book:

- Automatically stop with needle down

- Presser foot "hover" or knee lift - with needle down, presser foot can lift slightly to allow adjustments to the position of your project

- Quick change of presser feet and settings

- Adjustable stitch position – can shift a decorative stitch left or right to stitch in a different place

- Stitch memory – able to "save" favorite or commonly used stitches to recall later

- Presser foot pressure or height adjustment – helps when stitching thicker materials

Machine Presser Feet

Not all of these feet are required, but I have found each one helpful in performing a specific task. Your sewing machine feet may not look the same or have the same name, so I've tried to describe them well enough for you to find something close.

The good news is: you won't need a walking foot!

Narrow Zipper Foot

This type of foot is great for more than just zippers. The narrow profile and length allow you to hold more of the quilt surface when basting the edges of the top to secure it to the batting and backing.

Edge Stitching Foot

This foot features a metal guide on the right side of the foot and a wide opening for adjusting the needle position. Place your fabric to the left of the guide, and adjust your needle to the correct position.

Some versions of this foot also allow adjustment of the outside guide. Avoid guides placed in the center of the foot.

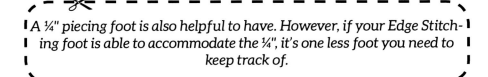

A ¼" piecing foot is also helpful to have. However, if your Edge Stitching foot is able to accommodate the ¼", it's one less foot you need to keep track of.

Left Edge Topstitch (Bi-Level) Foot

The right side of this foot is higher than the left side, making it perfect for accommodating the difference in height between the quilt top and binding. The left side rides along the edge; while the right side sits on top of the binding.

The needle opening on this foot needs to be wide enough to accommodate a zigzag stitch.

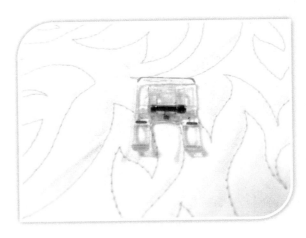

Clear Open Toe Appliqué Foot

In the event that a Left Edge Topstitch foot is not available, the Open Toe foot is the next-best option. Having fuller visibility of the stitching area allows you to have more control over stitch placement.

The metal version of this foot is also a good option.

What if specialty feet aren't available?

I used to do this method only with a ¼" piecing foot and an open toe appliqué foot. It's definitely doable!

The narrow zipper foot is only for basting the edges of the quilt. Technically, you can do that with any foot, but I like the zipper foot because it rides along the edge and I don't have to think about it.

The edge guide foot (at least the one I have) can be set up for pretty much any needle position. I like the guide on the far right because the thickness of the quilt sandwich rides next to the guide, so my stitches are more accurately placed.

The left topstitch foot was a relatively recent discovery. I like how the two heights on the foot allows the foot to ride next to the binding, so again, my stitches are more accurate.

But if all you have is a regular foot, you can still do this! It just might mean slowing down and guiding your project more firmly. Your technique will improve with either practice, with better tools, or both. Just don't let the perfect get in the way of the good.

Binding Control

These supplies aren't strictly required, but they do help with managing the binding throughout the process.

Binding Babies by Doohikey Designs

These are a fun and whimsical alternative to a simple cardboard tube or letting the binding puddle on the floor.

The medium and large sizes are most common for quilt binding, and they come in a variety of colors and hair styles.

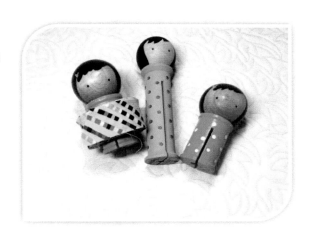

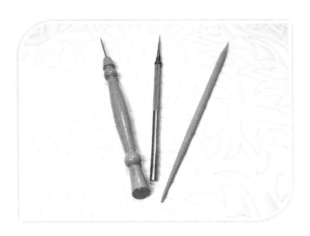

Dry Iron

This no-frills iron gets extremely hot, does not have an auto-shut off, and has a solid sole plate.

The solid sole plate and lack of moisture means no surprises with unexpected spots or debris falling onto the quilt when pressing.

Stiletto

Sometimes binding needs a little more control, and putting your fingers too close to the needle can be a dangerous option.

Stilettos come in metal, wood, plastic, and all combinations in between. The best ones fit comfortably in your hand and keep you at a suitable distance from the needle.

Part 2: Binding Basics

One of the first things I think about when working on my quilting projects is the method I want to use to bind my quilts. There are so many different ways to finish your quilts! You can face the edges, use single-fold binding, French-fold (double-fold) binding, turn the binding from the backing fabric, use prairie points — the possibilities are truly endless. We're going to focus on French-fold binding throughout the book; if you want to use single-fold binding instead, there are a few tips for modifying this method in *Part 8 - Frequently Asked Questions*.

Types of French-fold Binding

French-fold binding is made when you fold a strip in half lengthwise; you then stitch this folded strip to your quilt, aligning the raw edges, and finally turn the folded strip to cover the raw edges. This binding can be cut on either the crosswise grain, or the bias.

Crosswise grain runs from selvage to selvage, across the width of the fabric. Binding cut on this grain will stretch somewhat, and it makes the best use of fabric. However, it is not as durable as a bias cut binding. If the binding develops wear along the edge, it can rip along this line of wear, requiring replacement of the binding.

Bias binding runs at a 45° angle to the crosswise grain. It can stretch out of shape if you aren't careful, but that stretch is an ideal characteristic if you need to go around a curve. It's also the most durable binding you can make. Due to the diagonal crossing of the thread, if wear develops along the edge of the quilt, it just creates a hole in the binding rather than a rip, so it's much easier to repair.

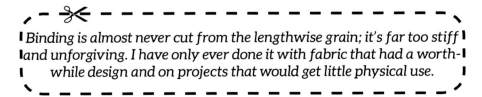

Binding is almost never cut from the lengthwise grain; it's far too stiff and unforgiving. I have only ever done it with fabric that had a worthwhile design and on projects that would get little physical use.

Many people think bias-cut binding doesn't use the fabric as efficiently as crosswise grain, but that's because so many instructions only tell you how to get bias binding from a square, instead of fully utilizing the fabric available.

Despite the obvious advantages of bias binding, I typically use it only for specific situations:

1. When my quilt edge is curved or irregular (bias binding will conform to the curve and lay flat when finished.)

2. When the quilt will get heavy usage (great for baby quilts and picnic blankets.)

3. When the fabric looks better or more interesting cut on the bias (stripes and plaids are especially fun.)

Otherwise, I cut my binding across the width of the fabric and don't give it another thought.

Calculate the Binding Strip Width

You can cut your binding at any width you want, but take into consideration the finished width of the binding you want to achieve. A proper binding is balanced on the front side and the back, with the edge of the quilt sandwich touching the inside of the binding all the way around. That's known as a "full" binding.

Unfortunately, I see a lot of quilters who just cut their binding at 2½", and stitch it with a ¼" seam allowance, regardless of what the quilt needs.

In reality, a 2½" cut binding generally yields a ⅜" finished binding, and stitching it with the wrong seam allowance can cause issues later when you're trying to make a neat finish. If you want a ⅜" finished binding - great, but if you wanted a ¼" finish instead, that 2½" cut binding won't always work to create a full binding.

A basic formula to use to calculate the cut width of your strips is:

(6 × FINISHED BINDING WIDTH) + (¼" to ½" EASE)

In French-fold binding, everything is doubled, so to get to (6) binding widths, you need to account for (2) seam allowances, (2) layers of binding on the front, and (2) layers on the back.

The extra ¼" to ½" of ease allows for the thickness of your batting and the little bit of fabric you lose in folding the binding over the edge of the quilt.

No matter what width you choose, it's important to trim your quilts correctly and set your machine to the correct seam allowance to make the binding look great.

Let's do a real example. Let's say I want a binding that finishes at ¼". How wide should I cut my strips?

(6 × ¼") + (¼" to ½" EASE) = 1½" + EASE = 1¾"– to 2"–WIDE CUT STRIPS

Wow! That's much narrower than the 2½" strips everyone cuts by default!

Also, if you have a very high-loft batting, you may need to adjust that ease measurement even more. This is why people find quilt binding so challenging: there are many variables to consider before you find the right combination that yields a full binding that looks amazing.

> *Once you learn the technique, I recommend making samples of your most commonly-used batting and fabric combinations, with the width of binding strip you want to use. You'll start to see where you need to make adjustments to get a full, balanced binding.*

Throughout the rest of the book, we will work with 2½" cut strips, since that is the most common, but I'll highlight where we need to make adjustments for this strip width to work in other scenarios.

Calculate the Binding Length

Of course there's a formula for calculating how much fabric you need for your binding, and it starts with knowing how much binding "length" is needed to go around the perimeter of your quilt. That formula for length is simply:

2 × (QUILT LENGTH + QUILT WIDTH) + 15" BUFFER

So for a quilt that's 50" x 60", your total length of binding needed is:

2 × (50" + 60") + 15" BUFFER = 2 × (110") + 15" = 235"

Now we just have to calculate how much fabric this will require. We need two numbers: the cut width of the binding strips, and the amount of usable fabric per cut. This same formula works for both crosswise and bias binding.

Determine the Fabric Required

For all fabrics, I assume that 40" is the usable amount of fabric (once the selvages are removed) when I cut across the width of the fabric. Knowing this, I can divide the length of binding I need by the usable fabric amount to find out the number of strips that need to be cut. So:

$$235" \div 40" = 5.88 \text{ strips or 6 strips}$$

Always round up to the next largest whole number, as we aren't going to work with partial strips.

To understand how much fabric is needed, you need to multiply the number of strips by the cut width of the strips, which gives you the width of the fabric in inches. This is rounded up to the nearest ⅛ yard. In our example:

$$6 \text{ strips} \times 2\frac{1}{2}" = 15", \text{ rounded up to } \frac{1}{2} \text{ yard (18")}$$

You should have no problem getting the amount of binding you need from the same amount of fabric, regardless of whether you are cutting crosswise or bias binding.

Below is a chart showing how much binding you can get from common cuts of fabric using 2½" cut strips. You can see that bias cutting is actually more efficient!

2½" Cut Strips

Yardage	Crosswise Binding Length Yield	Bias Binding Length Yield	Approximate Quilt Dimensions
Fat Quarter	110"	123"	27" × 27"
1/4 yard	110"	130"	27" × 27"
3/8 yard	180"	187"	45" × 45"
1/2 yard	250"	260"	62" × 62"
5/8 yard	320"	340"	80" × 80"
3/4 yard	355"	375"	88" × 88"
7/8 yard	425"	452"	106" × 106"
1 yard	495"	514"	123" × 123"

Calculations assume 40" of usable fabric after removing selvages (20" for a fat quarter)

Prepare the Binding Fabric

Whenever I cut strips, I make it a point to always straighten my fabric along the grain first. Fabric rarely comes perfectly aligned right off the bolt, so it takes a little bit of effort to make sure it is on-grain.

To straighten your fabric, first press out all wrinkles and especially the bolt-fold. You don't want this fold to make it difficult to see the true grain.

Hold up the fabric by the selvages, between your fingers, keeping the selvages straight along the top.

In this photo is an exaggerated way of showing that the fabric is not on-grain, even though the selvages are straight.

It's far too common to ask for yardage off the bolt and end up being shorted due to twisted grain!

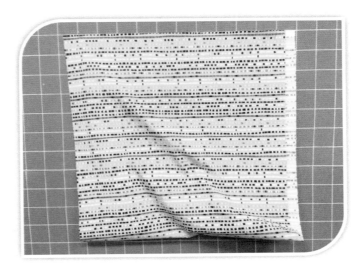

To see how far off your fabric is from being cut on-grain, hold the selvages together and align the cut edges on the left.

Notice here that with the cut edge aligned on the left, the fabric looks a little off-kilter and the folded edge is still twisted.

If we did not take the time to straighten the fabric first, our binding strips would also be twisted this way - giving the dreaded "V" or "W" shape.

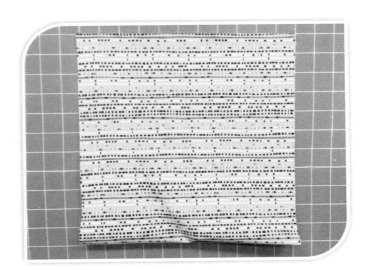

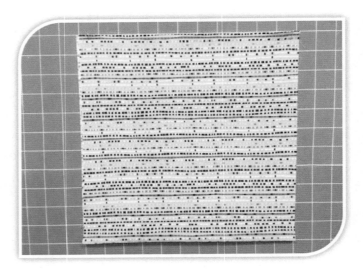

Keeping the selvages aligned, adjust the fabric until you see the twist go away and the fabric falls straight and even.

Your cut edges are no longer even, and that's okay. You've just straightened your fabric; now we have to square it!

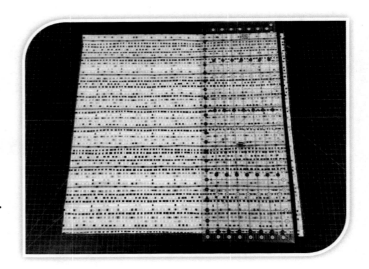

Lay your fabric on your cutting mat, preserving the straight-grain with the fold away from you.

Align your acrylic ruler with the fold and cut off one edge of the fabric (the side of your dominant hand) to make a new straight edge.

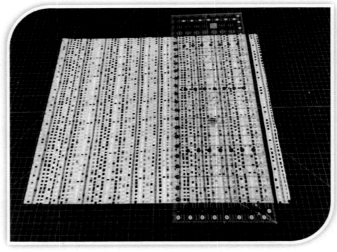

Now that you have a straight edge, rotate your fabric so that your straight edge is along the bottom and the selvages are on the side of your dominant hand.

Align your ruler with the straight edge and the fold and remove your selvages.

If you're making crosswise binding, you are ready to cut strips.

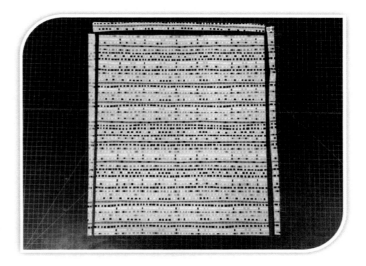

If you're making bias binding, you need to square the remaining cut side of the fabric.

Rotate the fabric until the remaining cut edge is on the side of your dominant hand.

Align your acrylic ruler with the fold and cut off the edge of the fabric to make a new straight edge.

Using Straight vs. Diagonal Seams

In the next couple of chapters, we'll be cutting and sewing binding strips from our cut yardage, but first a word about joining seams.

By far, the most common way of joining binding strips is with a diagonal seam. It is a strong join in addition to distributing the bulk of the seam, which makes it easier to stitch the binding by hand or machine.

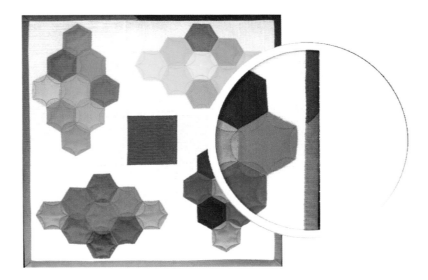

For aesthetic reasons, you may choose instead to use a straight seam join. It uses less fabric, and is great for pieced bindings where you want to place seams in an exact location or it serves the visual of the quilt better. We won't cover straight seam joins here, but just know it's an option if you prefer it! If you do choose straight joins, always press your seams open.

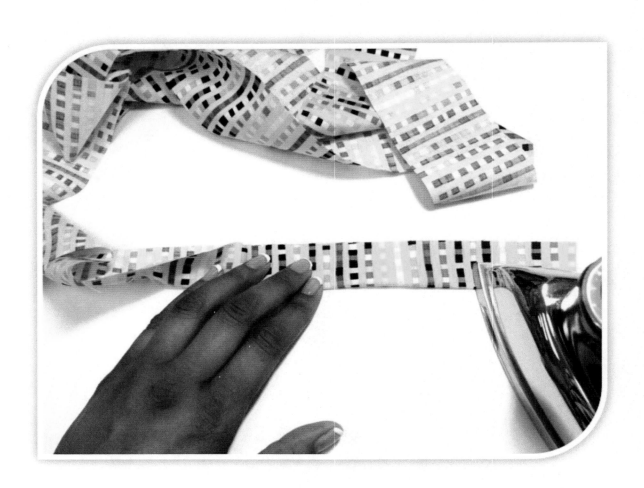

Part 3: Make Crosswise-Grain Binding

I've been making crosswise-grain binding forever, but it wasn't always as easy for me as it is now. When I first started quilting, I was taught to cut my binding at 2⅝". I found this to be such a fussy measurement that I almost gave up quilting!

Later on, I figured out how to make adjustments in other ways so I could use a more standard binding width, and since I first developed and perfected this technique, 2½" wide strips reign supreme. Ultimately, I want you to find the width that works for you and keeps you quilting, so don't be afraid to experiment as you learn.

Cut Crosswise Binding Strips

Rotate your fabric around so that the fold is toward you.

Align your ruler on the mark that represents your chosen strip width (2½" in our example.)

Continue cutting strips to your desired width until you get the total number of strips you need for your quilt.

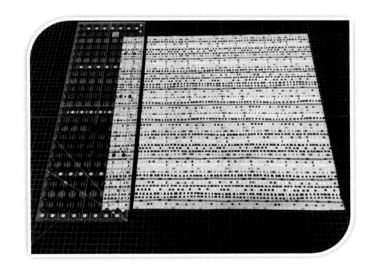

Sew Crosswise Binding Strips

Once you have all the strips you need, you need to connect them together to form one long strip. We're going to use a diagonal seam, so that the bulk is distributed over the width of the strip.

If you'd rather use a straight seam join instead, you can simply lay strips right sides together, stitch them with a ¼" seam allowance, and press the seams open.

To prepare a diagonal seam, lay out one binding strip, right side up, with the length trailing off to the left side.

Align a second strip, right side down, with the length trailing toward you, forming a square corner as shown.

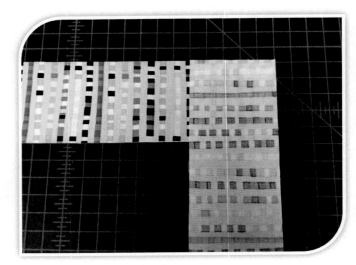

Using the LoveBug Studios Binding Tool, face up so the text is readable, align the tool with the square corner of your overlapped strips, so the dog-eared corner aligns with the right edge.

The bottom edge of the tool should match the strip facing up, and the binding width measurement will line up with the marked line on the ruler (or the top edge for 2½" strips).

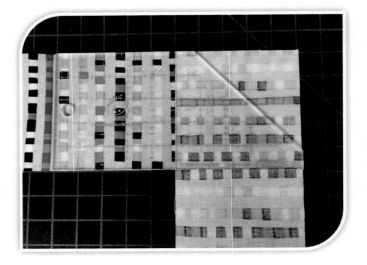

Part 3: Make Crosswise-Grain Binding

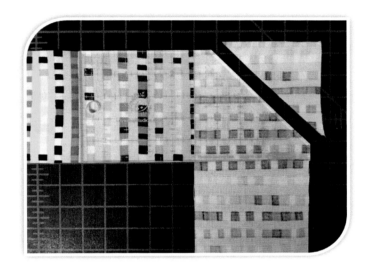

Cut off the exposed fabric to the right of the tool through both layers, and pin the strips together.

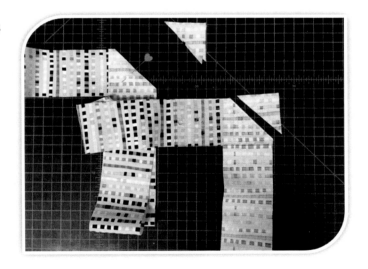

Take the free end of the strip that's facing down, and turn it so the right side is facing up with the previous pinned strips trailing off to the left.

Place the next strip, right side down, forming a square corner with the right side up strip.

Repeat the previous steps until you get all the binding seams cut and pinned.

Set up your machine to stitch a ¼" seam allowance.

Stitch all the diagonal seams in the binding.

Press Crosswise Binding Strips

For this step, you'll want a good pressing surface and a hot, dry iron.

Try to avoid using steam, water, or starch at this stage so you don't distort your binding fabric.

Press all the seams open to reduce bulk.

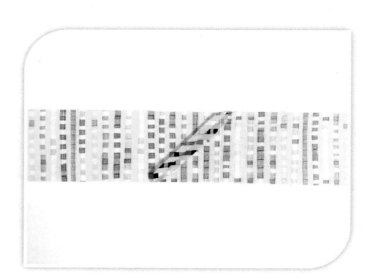

You can press all the seams open at once, or press them as you go. For my own process, I press as I go; it means handling the strips less, and that reduces the opportunities for distortion. Crosswise grain isn't as stretchy as bias, but it stretches enough to be a pain!

Part 3: Make Crosswise-Grain Binding

Fold the binding strip in half widthwise, right side out, and press along the length, being careful not to stretch or distort it.

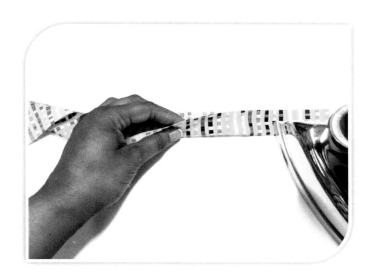

As you work, carefully wind the pressed binding around an empty cardboard tube or spool to protect it from stretching.

A fun way to store your finished binding is on Binding Babies®!

Part 4: Make Bias Binding

Bias binding is a little trickier to cut, because you need to cut at a 45° angle to get the true bias grain. There are several methods for doing this, and you can choose your method depending on how much time you want to spend on the effort!

One of the most popular methods of cutting bias binding involves drawing lines, stitching fabric into a twisted tube, and then cutting it all out along the drawn lines with a pair of scissors. While this certainly is a clever way to achieve continuous binding by stitching a single seam, you're not actually cutting on the true bias.

I will focus on the simplest method that's least wasteful of fabric and time. You'll have more seams to stitch, but you can use your rotary cutter the entire time!

Cut Bias Binding Strips

In **Part 2: Binding Basics**, we straightened and squared the fabric needed for bias binding, and now it's ready to cut.

Unfold your fabric onto a cutting mat with the wrong side up, and the former selvages to your left and right.

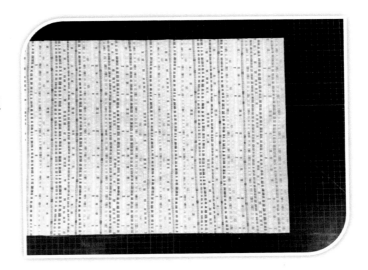

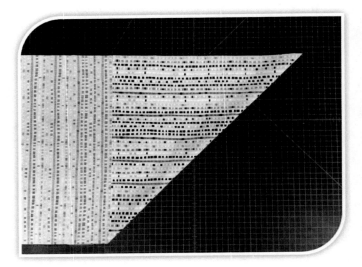

Fold the lower right corner up at an angle to meet the top raw edge. Lightly finger-press the fold.

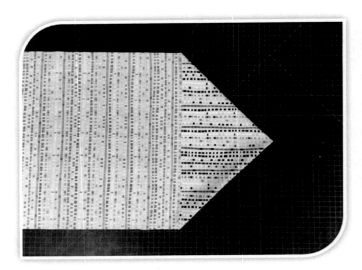

Fold the upper right corner down over the previous fold, matching points and the fold.

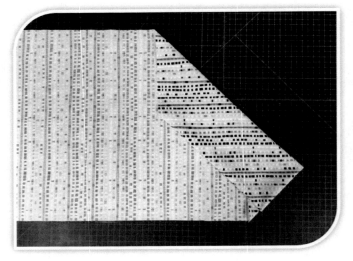

If you're working with a wider cut of yardage, you may need to fold the fabric again so it's able to be cut with your ruler.

To do this, fold down the upper right edge, keeping all the folds aligned.

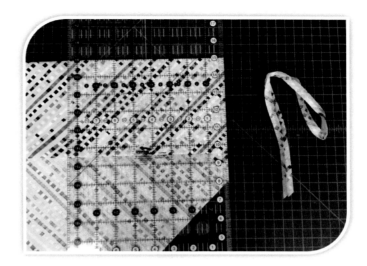

Rotate the fabric with the folds toward your dominant hand, keeping folds aligned.

Align your ruler close to the folded edge of the fabric, and cut off the tiniest sliver of fabric through all layers.

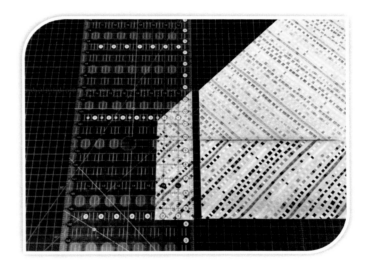

Rotate the fabric 180° so the bulk of the fabric is up toward your right.

Align your ruler on the mark that represents your chosen strip width (2½" in our example). Cut through all layers.

Continue cutting strips until the fabric is too small to reasonably work as binding, or until you reach a point where the fabric is longer than your ruler.

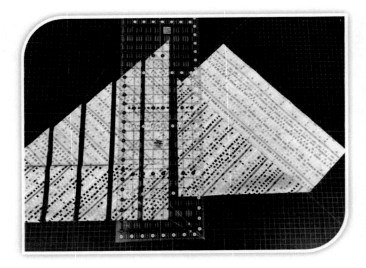

If needed, to continue cutting, fold the remaining fabric wrong sides together, keeping the cut edge aligned, until it fits into your ruler's cutting field.

Continue cutting strips in this manner until the fabric is too small to reasonably work as binding.

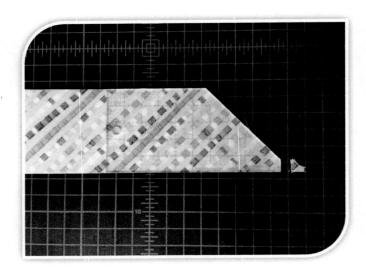

Stack several binding strips, carefully aligning the angled edges.

Using the LoveBug Studios Binding Tool, face up so the text is readable, align the tool with the angled side of each stack.

Cut off the exposed fabric to the right of the tool through all layers, to dog-ear the corners.

Sew Bias Binding Strips

Once all your strips are cut, you'll have two types of cut strips. Before you start sewing, you need to understand how to handle these so that you can get one continuous strip without having to re-cut any of the binding ends.

Type 1 strips will have the angled ends facing the same direction.

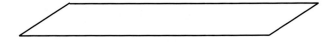

Part 4: Make Bias Binding

Sort these strips together. These will essentially be sewn end to end, so that their angles will match.

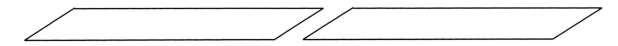

Type 2 strips will have the angled ends facing opposite directions.

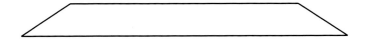

To stitch these, rotate every other strip, then sew them end to end, in order to get the angles to match.

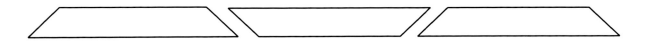

When you're stitching the strips, stitch each type together independently. For your final seam, you'll need to match one end of the Type 1 strip length with the corresponding end of the Type 2 strip length.

In the event that you need to re-cut one of the angled ends, you can use the Binding Tool to square off the end and re-cut it to the proper angle.

To stitch the strips together (either Type 1 or Type 2), lay them right sides together, so that they meet at a 90° angle, and the dog-eared corners match.

Set up your machine to stitch a ¼" seam allowance.

Stitch all the diagonal seams in the binding,

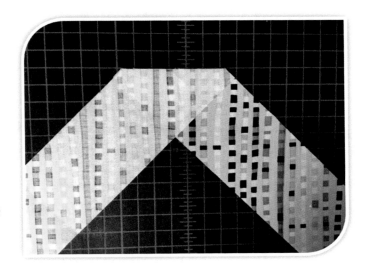

From here, you can follow the steps in **Part 3 - Press Crosswise Binding Strips.** The steps are the same, just be extra-careful not to stretch your strips.

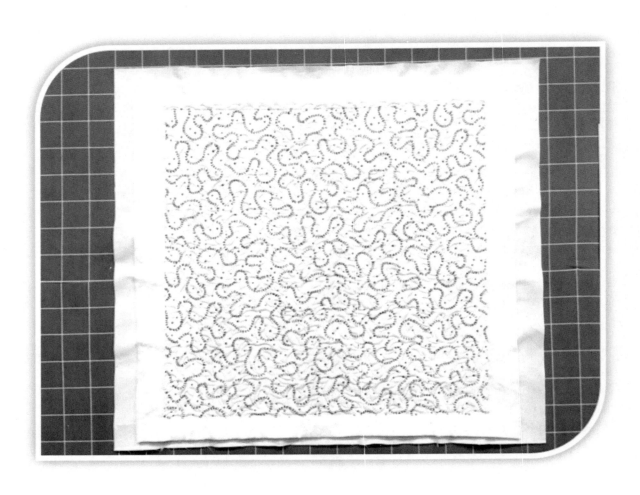

Part 5: Prepare to Bind the Quilt

Now that we've prepared our binding, we're almost ready to attach the binding to the quilt. This is where your results are going to vary, and the first time you do this, you'll want to conduct a couple of experiments to get the settings correct for your project. Your binding attachment will vary based on a few factors:

- Type of fabric (cotton, flannel, or plush)

- Type of batting (high, medium, or low loft)

- Type of quilt (pieced to the edge, with or without borders, etc.)

- Type of binding finish (decorative, zigzag, or straight)

If you change any of these variables, you'll need to repeat these steps to make sure you get the best results on each project.

Prep, Baste and Trim the Quilt

When you make a quilt, the batting and backing extend beyond the quilt top, and this will eventually need to be trimmed off. Before we do that, we need to prep, baste, and trim the quilt based on the type of quilt and look you want to achieve.

To prep the quilt, evaluate whether or not it needs to be blocked. Sometimes quilting can introduce wonkiness and waviness into the quilt so that it's no longer flat and square. If your quilt waves at you, your binding will too! The process to return the quilt to flat and square is called, "blocking".

Not all quilts require blocking; I typically only do this for quilts that will be hung to exhibit or need to be photographed. The quilt has to be dampened, measured and manipulated to make it flat and square, and then left to dry. You need a flat, clean, pinnable surface, and the time and space to do the blocking from start to finish.

If you need to learn how to block your quilt, check out the Resources chapter at the end of the book for further instruction.

The next step before we get to trimming is to baste your quilt to secure all the edges. If you have quilted on your domestic machine, you do this after the quilting is complete.

If your quilt was quilted on a long arm, it's likely this basting is already in place. If it isn't, check with your quilter to see if they will do this for you on your next quilt; the edge basting helps to keep your quilt straight and square on the frame.

If you need to add basting, use your zipper foot and the longest stitch length your machine allows (mine is 6.0mm).

Stitch around the edge of your quilt ⅛" from the edge of the quilt top, all around the perimeter (red dashed line).

Do this before trimming your quilt.

To trim the quilt, you'll need a large flat surface, a cutting mat, a long ruler, a large square ruler, and a rotary cutter. The long ruler will help you to keep the edges straight. The large square ruler can help you at the corners.

If your quilt does not have pieced angular or curved blocks out to the edge (where the seam allowance must be preserved so as not to cut off points or intersections), trim the batting and backing right next to the edge of the quilt.

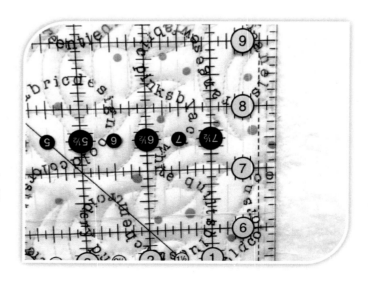

Spread out your quilt onto the cutting surface, extending the batting and backing away from the quilt. Align your ruler along the edge of the quilt top and trim away the excess batting and backing.

If your piecing goes out to the edge and you want to preserve your points and intersections, you can either:

Trim the quilt next to the edge, and cut your binding width to a size that is compatible with a ¼" seam allowance; or

Trim your quilt ⅛" from the edge of the quilt top, and cut your binding width to a size that is compatible with a ⅜" seam allowance.

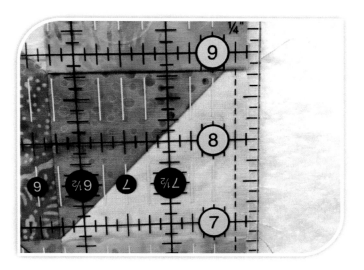

Test Machine Settings

Before we permanently attach the binding to the quilt, let's play with our machine settings so we stitch on the binding accurately. We want to make sure all the settings are correct, because in the final step, we're stitching from the front of the project and won't be able to see what's happening on the back.

Start with the Edge Stitching Foot or a Zigzag Foot. Set your machine to a long basting stitch using a contrasting thread, 75/11 needle, and with the needle to the far right (6.0mm is the stitch length; 3.5 is the right needle position on my machine.)

If your machine doesn't allow you to move the needle, use a bit of masking tape to mark a sewing guide on the bed of your machine.

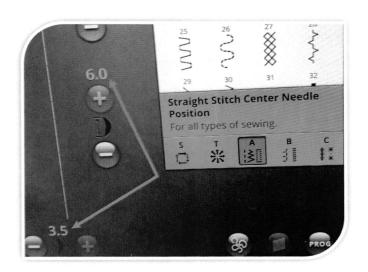

Do you use different battings or binding widths on your projects? It may be a good idea to make up some small samples so you can play with this technique. Use a permanent fabric pen to write down your settings on each sample; next time you use that combination, you'll already know what to do!

The exact measurement from the needle to the edge of the foot isn't as critical as being able to identify and replicate it once you get the right settings.

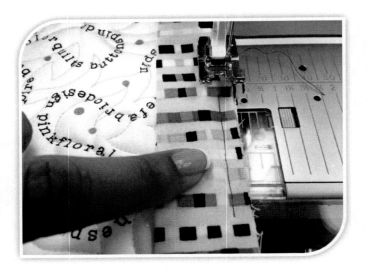

First, align the raw edge of the **front** of your quilt sandwich with the raw edges of your binding. Stitch 2-3" with the basting stitch and remove it from the machine.

The "where" doesn't matter; you'll likely be removing these stitches!

If you trimmed your quilt with the batting and backing flush with the edge of the quilt top, align the binding with this edge. If you trimmed the batting and backing a distance away from the quilt top, align the binding with the edge of the batting and backing.

Fold this test section to the back of the quilt and test the fit. You want the quilt sandwich to fill the binding without needing to yank on it. You also want the binding to slightly cover the stitches.

In this example, there is clearly too much extra binding turned to the back, so I need to move my needle (or my guide).

What we're trying to find here is the seam allowance that will give us the best balance of fabric on the front and the back, cover our stitching line, and look just as good on both sides of the quilt. **It should be close to, but may not be exactly, the finished binding width we calculated in Part 2.**

The above example is the typical one shown in magazines, tutorials, and videos everywhere: the 2½" binding strip stitched with a ¼" seam allowance. It's fine perhaps when you are hand stitching and can manipulate the binding to hide your stitches.

However, when you're stitching by machine, this will result in a binding that only looks good on one side. Pay close attention: these tutorials never show you what the back of the quilt looks like!

Whenever you're testing your binding attachment settings, too much fabric on the back indicates moving your needle left to take up more of the binding strip. Not enough fabric on the back indicates moving your needle right to take up less fabric.

Remove the basting stitches, and try again with a different needle position.

Since there is too much fabric turned to the back, I need to move my needle left.

In this example, the machine is still set to the 6.0mm basting stitch, but the needle has been moved left (all the way to the 0.0 center position.)

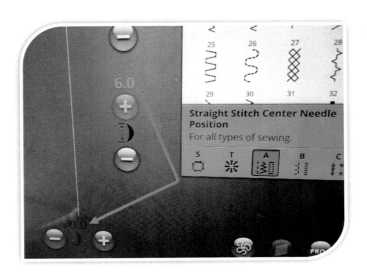

If you are testing your machine settings moving only right to left, you can leave your basting stitches in, because they won't interfere with your next test. The moment you move left to right, you must pull out the basting as it will prevent you from testing the next adjustment.

Again, align the raw edge of the front of your quilt sandwich with the raw edges of your binding. Stitch another 2-3" with the new setting.

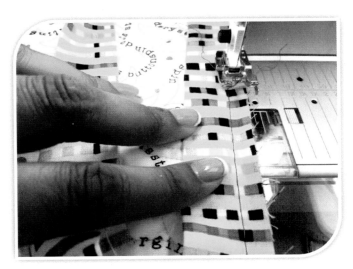

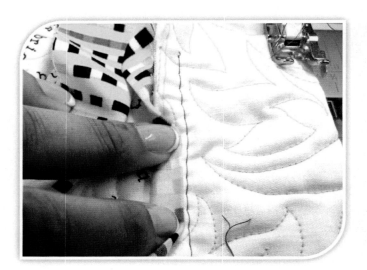

Fold this test section to the back of the quilt and test the fit.

In this example, there's not enough binding to cover the stitches. This means moving the needle (or the guide) to the right, to take up less fabric.

Continue adjusting your needle to the left or right until you get to a setting that works for the finishing method you plan to use.

In this example, the needle position has been moved to the right, to the 0.8 position.

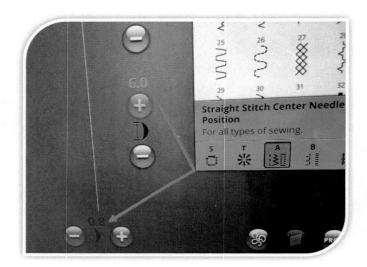

For a **zigzag finish**, you want your binding to just cover the stitching line on the back of the quilt, without having to pull or tug or stretch the binding to meet the stitching line.

For a **straight (in the ditch) finish**, the binding should go slightly past the stitching line, by no more than ⅛". For this technique to look good, you don't want a huge flap of binding on the back of the quilt.

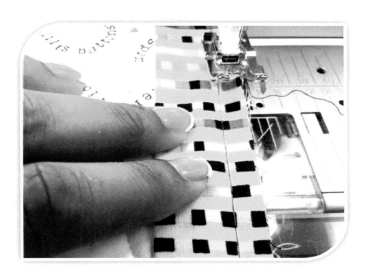

Once again, align the raw edge of the quilt sandwich with the raw edges of your binding. Stitch another 2-3" with the new setting.

Fold this test section to the back of the quilt and test the fit.

In this example, with the needle in the 0.8 position, the binding just covers the stitching line, which is perfect for using the zigzag stitch for finishing.

Every machine is different, as is every quilt. Don't assume your settings will be the same as mine. The point here is for you to understand, with your own sewing machine and your quilt in front of you, how to make adjustments to get your chosen binding to work. It may take more than 3 tries!

If instead of a 2½" binding strip, you decide to cut a 2" strip instead, you may find that the far right needle position is nearly perfect. The point is that only you will know for sure, and only by trying.

Write Down Your Needle Position:_____

Part 6: Attach Binding to the Quilt

It's the moment you've been waiting for! We've spent all this time building up to this point: attaching the binding to the quilt.

For this step, you'll need your prepared binding, a couple of pins, the Binding Tool, chalk, and thread that matches your binding. The closer in shade you get, the less your stitches will show.

Wind a bobbin, thread your machine, and let's do this.

Getting Started

With your perfect setting achieved (for either stitch in the ditch or a zigzag finish) reduce the stitch length from the basting stitch to one more appropriate – I use 2.0mm as the length. Change to a 90/14 needle. Your needle position should be set to what you wrote down in the previous chapter. Set your machine to stop with the needle down.

One of the cardinal laws of quilting states that for every four corners of binding you attach, one of them will have the seam of the joined binding strips in it.

You can avoid this by doing a dry-fit of the binding around the quilt. Position the starting tail of the binding along one side of the quilt, between the center of a side and the lower corner.

Pin the starting tail and then lay the binding around the quilt to see where the seams fall. If you see a binding seam coming close to falling in a corner, adjust the starting position of the binding to move the seams away from the corners.

This is just an audition; don't pin your binding around the quilt. Just let it roll off the spool or tube that you used to store it. You will have to rewind the binding of course, but the risk of skipping the audition is having a seam in your miter. It's up to you!

Start Stitching and Turn Corners

Start your stitching about 8" from the end of the binding tail that you pinned.

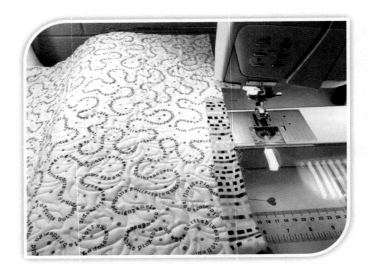

Align the raw edge of the quilt sandwich with the raw edges of your binding. Stitch 2-3" with your matching thread and remove the project from the machine.

Use the gridded corner of your Binding Tool to measure the distance from your stitching line to the edge of the quilt. Each dashed line represents ⅛". If your seam allowance is between the lines, consider marking the ruler with a bit of masking tape.

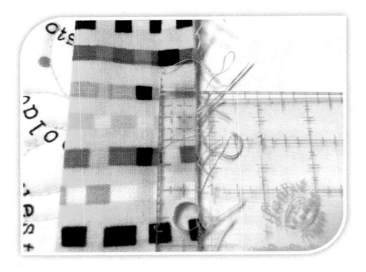

Part 6: Attach Binding to the Quilt

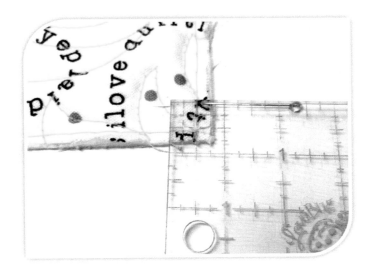

Move the Binding Tool to the first corner of your quilt; align your ruler on the quilt at the same distance from the corner as the stitching was from the edge of the quilt. Mark this point with a pin facing to the right.

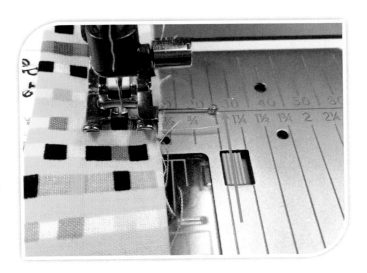

Place your project back in the machine, and continue stitching your binding up to the pin. Stop with your needle down at the pin.

On most modern sewing machines, your throat plate has a horizontal line which is in line with the needle. If you're having a hard time seeing where the needle is relative to the pin, just sew until the pin is over this horizontal line.

Pivot the quilt clockwise so the corner is directly in line with the needle. Stitch toward the corner to the end, stop, and clip your threads.

This very simple step is going to help you get your mitered corner correct.

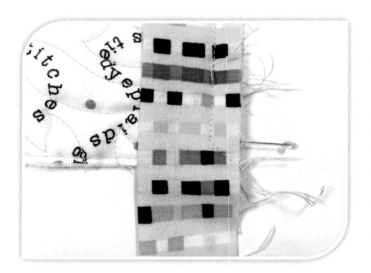

Note how you have a straight stitch, and then an angled stitch at the bottom off to the corner.

Use that angle as a guide to fold the binding back over your stitching line at the corner, so that the raw edge of your binding forms a straight line with the raw edge of your quilt.

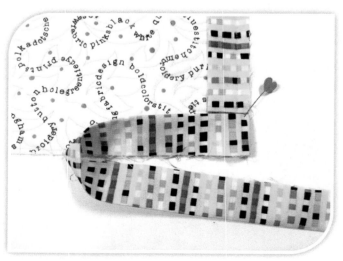

Fold the binding down so it covers the next side of the quilt and the fold is even and square with the edge of the quilt. Pin the corner in place.

Even and square. I can't repeat that enough. Take the time to make sure your fold here is even and square. Otherwise, your corner won't turn properly.

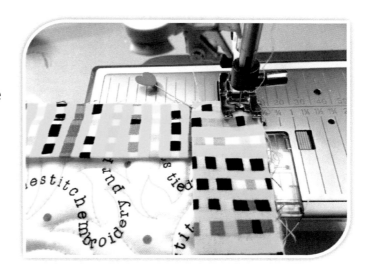

Starting from the folded edge of the binding, continue stitching the binding to the quilt in this manner.

When you get to the next corner, repeat the steps for marking and folding each corner.

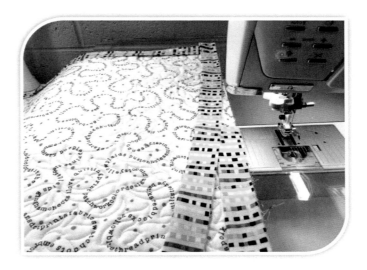

Keep stitching until you've completed the remaining 3 corners and you're about 10-12" from the beginning of your binding tail.

Stop stitching and remove the quilt from your machine.

Lay your quilt on your cutting surface, with the binding tails facing you. The starting binding tail should be flat on the quilt (blue arrow) and the other, longer tail, loose.

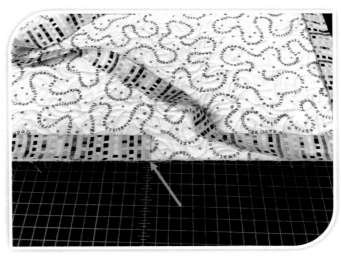

If you made bias binding, this starting tail should be angled already and dog-eared. Treat the straight edge of that dog-ear as the starting point of your binding (the blue arrow would be in the same position.)

Connect the Binding Tails

Connecting the ends of your binding is a little daunting the first time you do it, but you'll be a pro at it in no time at all.

I've found that by doing this the same way every time, I've built a routine that makes this process almost automatic and I'm no longer frustrated by twisted connections or miscut seams.

If you are left-handed, you can follow the instructions in whatever way is comfortable and safe for you. I've tried to note where you can make adjustments for cutting.

If this is your first time connecting binding ends this way, I suggest reading through the instructions first before cutting your actual project.

Overlap the loose tail over the starting binding tail. Using the square side of the Binding Tool, align the measurement of the cut width of the binding (or the right edge if it's 2½") with the end of the starting binding tail (marked by the blue arrow, underneath the loose tail.)

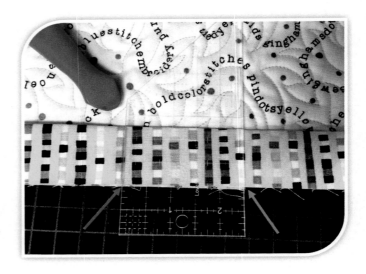

Using a chalk marker, mark the left edge of the binding tool directly onto the binding (red arrow.)

You are cutting the tail of the binding so that it is ⅛" shorter than your marking.

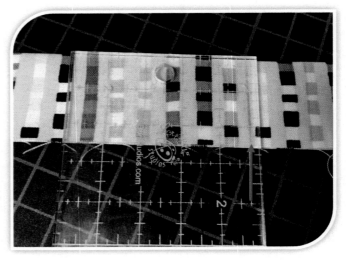

To do this, lay the loose tail of the binding flat on the cutting surface. Align the ⅛" mark of the Binding Tool on the chalk line you drew (red arrow), so that the chalk line will get cut off with the excess tail.

Part 6: Attach Binding to the Quilt

In this photo, the extra binding tail is cut off on the left (with the chalk mark) and the binding needed to finish the quilt is on the right.

This step helps to adjust slightly for the inevitable stretching that happens as you finish this last seam, and ensures a well-fitting binding with no tucks!

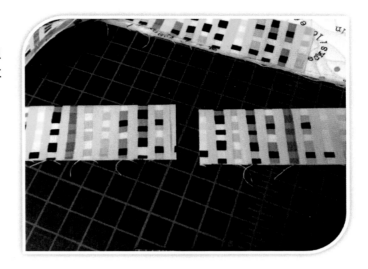

Rotate your quilt so that the open ends of the binding face your dominant hand.

Open up the binding tails and lay them flat, right side up, on your cutting surface. Do not twist them or flip them, just open them flat.

If you are working with bias binding and one of your tails is already angled, **SKIP THE NEXT STEP.**

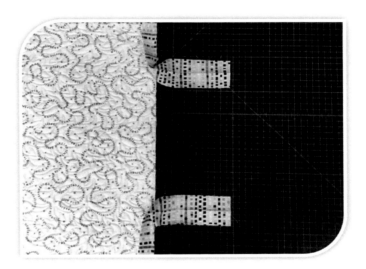

Using the LoveBug Studios Binding Tool, face up so the text is readable, align the tool with the square corner.

Align the bottom edge of the tool with the strip facing up, matching the top edge (or measurement line) with your binding width measurement, and aligning the right edges.

(If you are left-handed, this will be upside down when you do it.)

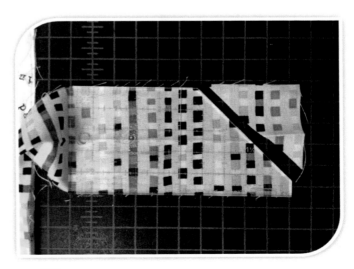

For the remaining end of the binding, you want to cut the other tail in exactly the same orientation.

If you were working with bias binding and one of your tails is already dog-eared, place the ruler in the same orientation as that tail.

(If the angle runs top-left to lower right, the text on the binding tool is readable. If the angle runs top right to bottom left, flip the ruler upside down.)

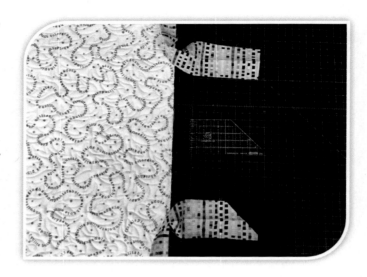

Align the ruler with the uncut binding tail and cut off the exposed corner.

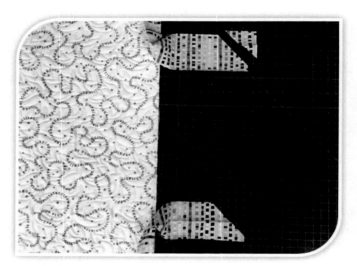

The diagonals on both ends of the binding should look exactly the same when you are finished.

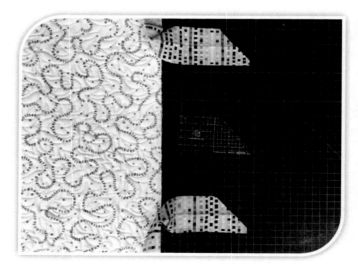

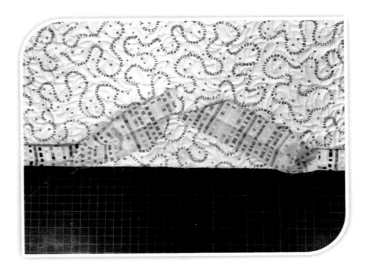

Rotate the quilt back toward you so the open ends of the binding are facing you.

Flip the binding tails so they are wrong side up. Don't twist them, just lay them wrong side up.

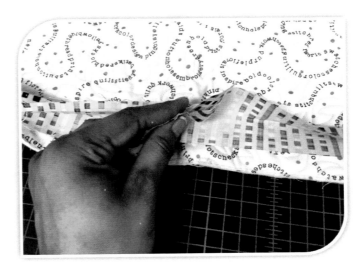

Pick up the two binding tails and bring them right sides together. You will need to maneuver your quilt out of the way.

Pin the tails right sides together.

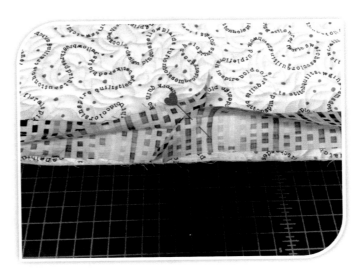

Check your work before you sew! If you release the pinned tails, you should see the binding in a straight line against your quilt without a twist.

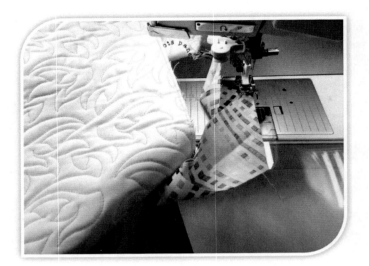

Take this back to your sewing machine. Change the needle position to sew a ¼" seam, and stitch this final seam to connect the ends of your binding.

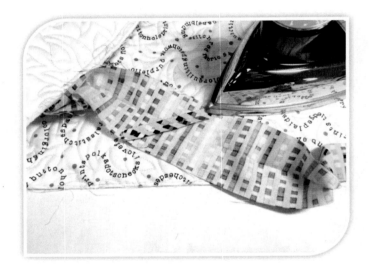

Press the seam open.

Change the needle position back to the setting it was on to stitch your binding. (You did write that down, didn't you?)

Finish stitching the binding to the quilt. If it feels like your binding is a little bit snug, don't worry; your machine will ease in your quilt and the binding will fit perfectly.

With a hot iron from the front of your project, press the binding to set the seam, and then press the binding away from the quilt.

This will give you a nice, crisp, even fold.

Now that wasn't so bad, was it? At this point, many people would just pull out a hand needle and finish it by hand, but not us. We're going to finish this quilt by machine.

In the event you do want to finish by hand, or you want to learn how to bind non-square corners, check out my other book!

Binding Crazy Angles

Mastering Curves, Points, Cleavage, and More

Ebony Love

bindingcrazyangles.com

Part 7: Finish the Binding

You're in the home stretch! You have a little more work to do, but you're very close to being finished. All that's left to do is choose your finishing stitch, and go to it!

Pin the Binding

I'll bet you were wondering how we were going to secure the binding and make sure it was finished neatly and didn't move. My answer to that is: pins!

The pins I use aren't just any pins; they are extra-fine, glasshead patchwork pins. What I love so much about these pins is that they are super-sharp — they glide smoothly in and out of the fabric. They are also thin enough that they don't distort the fabric being pinned.

I also sew over these pins on a regular basis. I know, we've all been taught not to sew over pins, but by keeping the pins in place as we sew, the binding doesn't move.

If you do hit a pin, a couple of things could happen:

- You'll slightly nick the pin, introducing a bit of a bend;

- You'll hit the pin and mangle it; or

- You'll hit the pin in the perfect spot and break it.

I've mangled a few pins over the years, and when it happens it can be scary, but I just stop sewing, take out the mangled pin, and keep going. These pins are so thin that they give way under the force of the needle (which is what you want), unlike other pins that can break a needle and throw off your machine timing.

You can continue using some of the bent pins or bend them back into a reasonable enough shape to do so; if they are bent too badly or have a rough spot, throw them away. (I collect them into an empty prescription bottle.)

To begin pinning, start along one side and fold the binding back over your stitch line. If you're planning to use a zigzag stitch to finish, just cover the line of stitching; if you want to use a straight stitch, your binding will overlap this line. Don't tug too hard, just fold it over so the raw edges of your quilt fill the binding space.

Insert a pin into the finished edge of the binding, trying to pin only through the binding and backing.

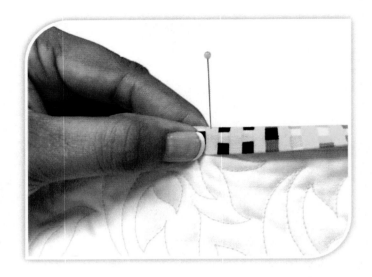

Rock the pin forward so that the tip of the pin exits just above the lower fold.

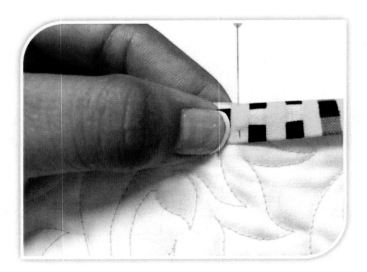

Rock the pin backward through the lower fold, catching the fold of the binding with the pin.

Tuck the point of the pin into the batting. You'll appreciate this later!

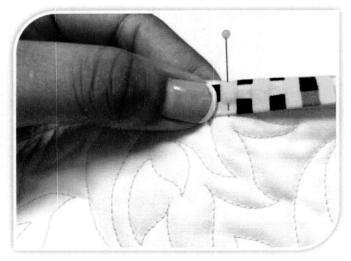

Part 7: Finish the Binding

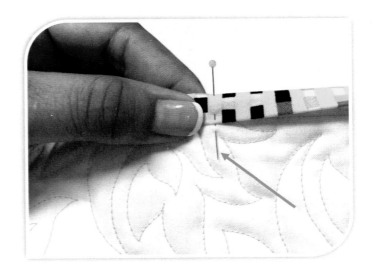

Don't leave the ends of your pins exposed like this. You only have to stab yourself a couple of times to appreciate how tucking in the points will help you.

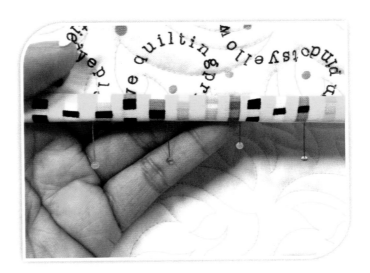

Continue pinning from the back side, placing your pins about 1" apart.

When you look at your pinning from the front of the quilt, there should not be any distortion from the pins.

This is good pinning. The binding is straight and isn't being pulled out of shape.

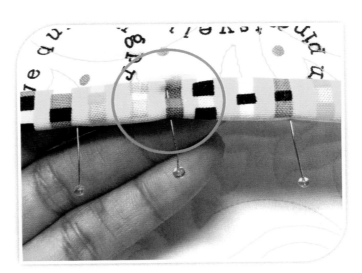

This is problem pinning. You can see the pin on the front of the quilt, and the binding is being pulled out of shape.

Continue pinning until you get to the corner. Insert a pin close to the corner, but not right in the corner.

Flatten the corner by pulling on the free edge of the binding near the corner. It will look like a triangle; this is the first half of your miter.

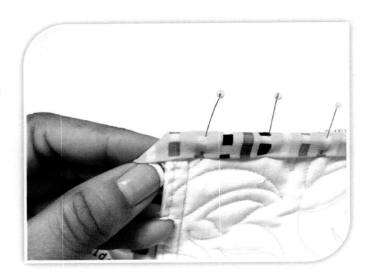

Bring the free edge of the binding toward the quilt. Fold your mitered corner and hold it in place between your thumb and forefinger.

Your corner should fold neatly and easily, without needing to clip out any layers from the corner. If the miter doesn't quite meet, try the fold again; you may need to pinch the first half of the miter to keep it from moving while you manipulate the free edge.

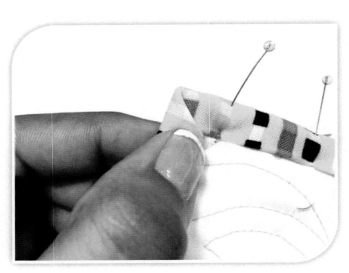

Weave a pin through the corner to secure it.

It may take a little practice to get this right, but try to pin through as few layers as possible and make sure your stitching line is covered completely.

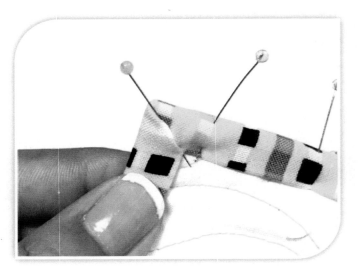

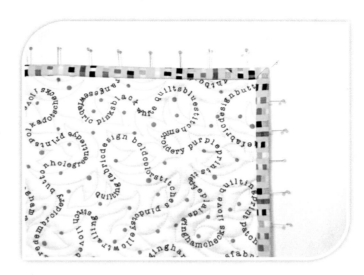

Continue pinning the rest of the quilt until the binding is completely secure, or until you run out of pins.

Basic Finish Using a Zigzag Stitch

What I love about the zigzag stitch is that it adds a little bit of personality to the quilt without worrying about the complexity of a more decorative stitch. As an added benefit, if you use a thread color that matches your binding, the zigzag stitch will just blend right into the stitching.

I can't tell you how many times this fast binding technique has saved me on a short deadline. It may not be the right technique if you're trying to get your quilt to win a national title, but it has served me well for magazine projects, photo shoots, and quilt exhibitions. If this technique is good enough for a magazine cover, anyone should be able to use it without guilt!

Set your machine to a narrow zigzag with a medium length. Here, my zigzag is 3.0mm long and 2.0mm wide.

You may need to do some test stitching to get this to your liking, but once you have the zigzag the way you want it, write down the setting and keep it with your machine so you always have it handy.

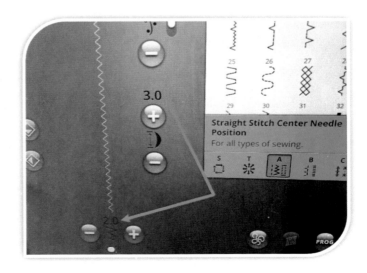

This setting may be different for you, not only because of your machine, but because what you find visually pleasing may be different from what I like. You may not like the zigzag at all, but prefer a different stitch. Don't be afraid to experiment!

Using your left edge topstitch or open toe appliqué foot, begin stitching with your needle down in the ditch next to the binding, with the quilt top face up.

The left position of your needle should just catch the binding on the back, and the right swing of the stitch will be right on top of the binding.

That way, even if your left stitch misses the binding, the right swing will catch it!

✂ -

Some sewing machines have the ability to adjust not only the stitch length and width, but also the stitch position. If you're using a left-edge topstitch foot and your zigzag seems out of alignment with the foot, check to see if you can make an adjustment to the stitch position.

Write Down Your Stitch Length:_____

Write Down Your Stitch Width:_____

Write Down Your Stitch Position:_____

Write Down Your Stitch Type:_____

Part 7: Finish the Binding

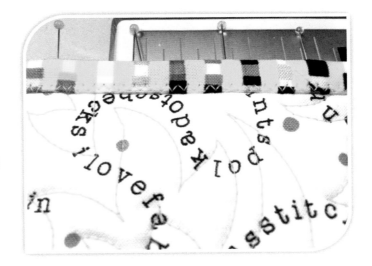

Before you stitch too far, check your stitches and make sure you've pinned securely enough to keep the binding in place.

So far it looks good from the front!

Check out the back while you're at it.

Who can even tell you were stitching blindly? Now this is a finish you can be proud of.

As you approach the corner, stitch past it, onto the miter, and stop with the needle in the right position.

Pivot the quilt and begin stitching the next side.

If you ran out of pins before getting to the rest of the quilt, this is a good place to pause, remove the pins from areas you've already stitched, and use them in places you still need to stitch.

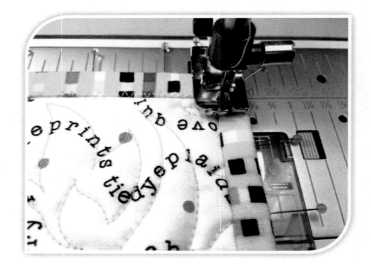

If you pinned this properly, you should have caught enough of the corner miter to keep it secure.

If your corner is not secure, you can remove a few inches of stitching and try again, or secure it with hand stitching.

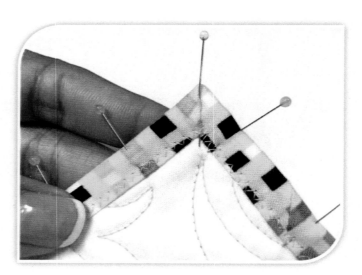

Do you love a crisp corner as much as I do?

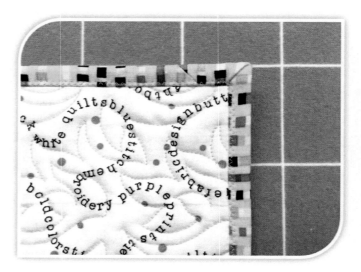

Part 7: Finish the Binding

Now that I've perfected this technique, I can't tell you the last time I completed a quilt binding by hand. Binding is a pleasure to do now instead of a pain. I love making miles and miles of binding, and having a marathon session stitching them on to quilts. I can bind several large quilts a day now, instead of only one.

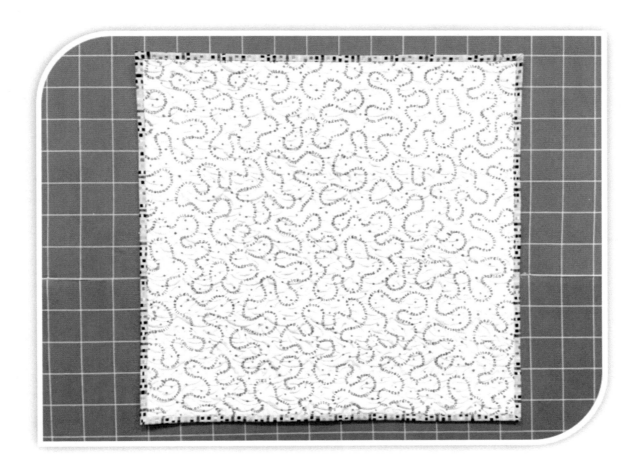

Advanced Finish Using a Straight Stitch

This technique isn't for the instant-gratification types. It takes patience and practice to master this method, but for those who do, you'll be rewarded with a beautifully finished binding that people will swear you hand-stitched until they look at the back.

When you set up for stitching in the ditch, the steps are very similar except for a couple of key differences:

1. Use a bobbin thread that matches your binding and a top thread that matches your quilt top (or monofilament if your top changes colors near the binding edge.)

2. Set your machine for a straight stitch that is slightly longer than what you would use for piecing.

3. When you pin your binding to the back, your binding should cover your stitching line a bit more than you would have used for the zigzag finish.

4. Place your pins closer together than you would for zigzag.

5. Check your stitching more often; it's easy to miss the binding and you don't want to get too far before noticing.

When this technique is done properly, it looks very professional and gives a nicer finish that's closer to hand-stitching (at least on the front).

Here, a contrasting thread color was used to illustrate the technique. This is the back side of the binding.

Part 7: Finish the Binding

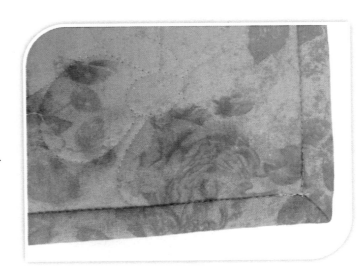

Here is the same project from the front (using contrasting thread). Note how the stitching nearly disappears when it is stitched exactly in the ditch.

To be perfectly honest, I'm still working on the straight stitching technique myself! The zigzag binding works so well that I rarely have a need for anything different, so practicing this is very low on my list of priorities. Many quilters wouldn't even attempt this without glue.

If this straight stitch technique is something you want to get great at, you have to practice, and that can involve a lot of awful-looking binding before you get good enough to be consistent.

Of course, I don't want this to sound like a judgment of you or the quality of your work; I just suspect that if you've purchased this book, and gotten this far, you're probably like me in a lot of ways. You want to finish faster, but you still want it to look amazing, and if you wanted something fussy that would take longer and didn't look as good, you might as well stitch it by hand.

Don't get me wrong; the zigzag finish does also take practice, but the learning curve is much less steep. You'll be able to get good at it pretty quickly, and use it for so many projects faster. My best advice? Baby steps. Try it the basic way, see how you like it, and if you want more of a challenge, move on to the straight stitch version.

I hope you've enjoyed learning this technique, and I wish you many happy hours binding your quilts successfully by machine. Best of luck, and happy quilting!

Part 8: Further Resources

There are so many things on the Internet, and so much more since I published the first edition of this book! I've tried to condense this to the best of the best, but nothing sits still on the Internet long enough to be immortalized in a book. I invite you to visit:

bindingbymachine.com

for updates, additional resources that couldn't be included here, plus interactive content. If you need working links for any of the products listed, you'll find those here too.

Where to Purchase

For the most part, I try to use commonly-available tools, but what's common in my sewing room and local shops isn't necessarily common everywhere!

I encourage you to shop your local independent retailer first, then your small online retailer (like me!), and as a last resort, try the big box, mass market retailers. When you shop small, and spend your money locally, you support your local community and keep our neighborhoods thriving!

LoveBug Studios – http://lovebugstudios.com

- Patchwork Pins
- Schmetz Quilting Needles
- Binding Tool
- Aurifil Thread (some colors)
- Chalk Liner Pen (yellow only)

Doohikey Designs – https://doohikeydesigns.com/

- Binding Babies

For other supplies such as machine presser feet, please visit your local sewing machine retailer. Most machine manufacturers have a foot or accessory catalog that you can view on-line. Many of the major brands have versions of the recommended feet in their catalog.

Videos and Classes

Need a quick refresher?

Years ago, I had a chance to tape several episodes with Mary Fons on her show *Quilty*, where we demonstrated this binding technique. Her show is no longer on the air, and we didn't get to show everything in these episodes, but they are perfect for a few tips.

https://www.quiltingcompany.com/how-to-make-quilt-binding-part-1/

https://www.quiltingcompany.com/how-to-attach-binding-to-a-quilt-part-2/

https://www.quiltingcompany.com/quilt-binding-with-turning-techniques-part-3/

Do you die cut?

If so, you might be interested in learning how to cut bias strips using your die cutter.

https://youtu.be/mItQREJSs30 (demonstrated using an AccuQuilt Studio cutter)

https://youtu.be/gueOpCryEj0 (demonstrated using an AccuQuilt GO! cutter)

Need to know how to block a quilt?

https://leahday.com/pages/how-to-block-a-quilt (Leah Day)

http://www.kimmyquilt.com/blocking-a-quilt.htm (Kimmy Brunner)

Need an in-person or virtual class?

I travel around the country teaching this technique to hundreds of students a year, and will begin offering an on-line class on my website so I can reach more students. Check this link for upcoming in-person and virtual classes.

https://lovebugstudios.com/classes/binding-by-machine/

Frequently Asked Questions

How do you choose thread to match the binding if the fabric is many colors?

First, I look to see if there's any single color that's dominating, or will appear more along the edge where I'll be stitching - like a background fabric.

If that doesn't work, I pick a color from the binding itself; something that blends, but doesn't stick out too much. Check out the cover photo for examples.

As a last resort - pick something wild! If you can't beat 'em, blind 'em is what I say. Pick something wacky and unexpected, like metallic.

No matter what, I audition several colors by unspooling a few inches of several color choices and pick from there.

What's been really helpful for me is having enough variety of thread to choose from. In the beginning, I got a thread color card from Aurifil, and I would pick 2 or 3 spools of thread to try and order a small spool of each - the 200m spools are less than $5.

But it's kind of like fabric - you have tons of it and it's never the right color!

Over time, that's settled down quite a bit - I make a lot of quilts with similar colors.

I do try not to use monofilament; it's not good to use for both top and bobbin thread (the threads don't lock) so you still have to find a matching thread anyway.

Can you use this technique with a flanged binding?

Absolutely! One of the cover quilts has a flange. The caveat here is the flange needs to be applied separately, not those mock flanges.

The reason is because to do a mock flange binding, you need to stitch your binding to the back, and turn it to the front. The technique in this book has binding stitched to the front and turned to the back. So if you want a flange, it needs to go onto the quilt first, then stitch your binding on top of it, and then follow the instructions to stitch either the zigzag or straight stitch.

Can I use a 40wt thread instead?

For attaching the binding, I would stick with 50wt, so you don't impact your seam allowance calculation. For the final stitching, use whatever you want!

Can you REALLY use this binding technique in a judged show?

The story I told in the introduction absolutely happened. But in all serious-ness... it was a nice comment from ONE judge, and personally I don't think the world of competition quilts is ready for machine binding.

Here's the thing: if you want to win, you can't give any judge a ready reason to deduct points. If your quilt is equally good to the other competition, except you did machine binding and someone else did hand binding, they may give the edge to the hand-binder.

If your quilts are equal, and you both did hand binding, but the other person also stitched their miters closed, the edge may go to that person.

I once got a first place ribbon because I was the only one who bothered to put a sleeve on my entry, and everyone else was disqualified.

If you want to win, don't give them a reason to make you lose. If you just want feedback and critique, try it and see what happens — and don't forget to tell me!

How do you make a scrappy binding?

Just stitch your strips together! You only need to decide whether you want to use diagonal seam or straight seam joins (see *Part 2 - Binding Basics*).

Straight seams are the easiest, but they do add bulk and can be harder to stitch. If you don't have too many seams it's not a huge issue, but if you wanted a bind-ing made from 2" squares, you'll have a harder time of it. I think I did that once, and ended up not using the binding, because there were just too many seams.

If you use diagonal seams, you need to make sure your pieces are long enough so that your diagonal seams don't overlap each other. With a 2½" cut strip for example, I wouldn't use pieces shorter than 6-8".

And the more seams there are, the more likely it is that at least one of your cor-ners will have a seam in it. Other than that, scrap away!

Does the width/size of your stitch change with different widths of binding, or do you keep the stitch the same?

I keep the stitch the same. In most cases, I don't want the binding threads to be obvious, so I keep them as low profile as possible.

The goal for me is to just make sure I securely catch the binding on the back, so I use a stitch that's wide enough to accomplish that without going too far into the actual binding.

Can you use this technique for single-fold binding?

I don't normally do single-fold binding, but this is entirely possible, with a couple of modifications.

The math for calculating your binding width is going to be different; instead of (6) finished widths plus ease, you'll only need (4) binding widths plus ease.

When you stitch your binding to the quilt, you'll stop for corners, miter, and connect your ends in the same way.

When you turn your binding to the back, it's the same process you would use for hand stitching, however, you'll need to experiment with your ease measurement for the cut width of the binding. Ideally, you want to be able to fold the raw edge of the binding to touch the raw edge of the quilt, and then when you fold the binding to the back, the fold just touches your line of stitching for zigzag (or just past for straight stitching.)

Your miters are folded the same way as you would for hand stitching.

What's the best and easiest way to make the corners even and flat?

Most people have problems with the corners of their binding because they aren't stopping in the right place, they aren't using a consistent seam allowance, or they don't fold their corner at the correct angle.

It's important to stop the same distance from the corner as the seam allowance you're using to stitch the binding to the quilt. That's what gives you a square corner.

You can also have issues if you try to fold the miter in the opposite direction. This often makes people think their corner is too bulky so they have to clip it, when really the miter just has to be folded the other way.

There's a section in *Chapter 6 - Start Stitching and Turn Corners* that covers this.

How do I miter corners on hexagons or other shapes? What about curves?

That's a different book in my binding series. It's called **Binding Crazy Angles.** That teaches binding by hand, but deals with inside and outside corners, acute and obtuse angles, and curved edges. With both books, you'll be unstoppable!

Get It Done Now! Binding a Quilt by Machine
2nd Edition

© 2019 Ebony Love. All rights reserved.

Every effort has been made to insure the accuracy of information in this publication; should you find any errors, please let us know at the address below and we will post corrections on our website.

Published by:

LoveBug Studios
1862 E. Belvidere Rd. PMB 388
Grayslake, IL 60030

http://lovebugstudios.com

ISBN 978-1-938889-19-6

Library of Congress Control Number 2019911204

Printed in the United States of America (US Distribution)

2 3 4 5 6 7 8 9 10

Made in the USA
Coppell, TX
26 December 2023

26859629R00045